Listening
Comprehension
Upper

Activities to improve listening skills

Written by Graeme Beals
Published by Prim-Ed Publishing

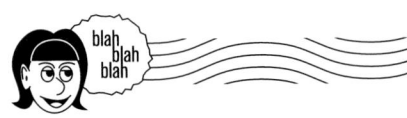 

Teachers Notes

The ability to listen with understanding is a major key to educational success. In fact, there is a very close correlation between listening ability and IQ scores.

The activities in **Listening Comprehension** are designed as teaching tools to build the listening skills of pupils. The activities are arranged to become progressively more difficult. It is expected that completion of two or three activities a week for approximately a month to six school weeks will gradually raise the listening vocabulary and concentration level of the pupils.

The activities can also be used as evaluative materials to identify problem areas and assess the development of pupils' listening skills. The graph sheet at the back of the book allows pupils to record each activity's results, providing immediate feedback on their listening skill development. It is suggested that the vocabulary difficulties pupils have also be recorded, so these can be addressed in general teaching. Ensure the pupils know the exercises become a little harder so they do not feel unduly bad if their scores deteriorate slightly.

Contents

Exercise One	1
Exercise Two	3
Exercise Three	5
Exercise Four	7
Exercise Five	9
Exercise Six	11
Exercise Seven	13
Exercise Eight	15
Exercise Nine	17
Exercise Ten	19
Exercise Eleven	21
Exercise Twelve	23
Graph Sheet	25

Exercise One

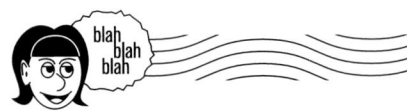 

Each pupil has a sheet of blank paper in front of him or her.

The teacher reads out each instruction twice.

Allow time between each instruction for the pupils to complete the required task(s).

It is useful if the pupils can not see one another's papers. However, it does not matter greatly as some instructions require different responses from different pupils.

Instructions:

1. Write your first name and the first letter of your middle name, at the top of the page, in the middle.

2. If you have black hair, draw a cross through your first name only.

3. If you are wearing anything blue, write the capital letter 'B' under your name. Otherwise, put a lower case 'd'.

4. Fold your page in half horizontally. Reopen it and on the back of your page, rule over the fold line.

5. Turn back to the front. In the lower half of the page, draw three circles arranged in the shape of a triangle, but not touching.

6. Using the letters 'X', 'Y' and 'Z', place one letter in the centre of each circle.

7. Inside the circles, place a circle around the letter 'X', a triangle around the 'Y', and a square around the 'Z'.

8. In the upper half of the page, draw a curved line which starts at the upper left-hand corner, comes down to touch the fold mark in the middle of the page, and then rises up to the top right-hand corner.

9. In the middle of the curve, draw four triangles, one within the other.

10. Outside the curve but within the top half of the page, draw two squares, one on each side near the base of the curve.

Exercise One

1. First name and first letter of second name.
2. If have black hair, cross through name.
3. 'B' here if wearing blue, otherwise 'd'.
4. Fold mark ruled on back.
5. Circles arranged in triangle shape.
6. 'X', 'Y' and 'Z' in circle centres.
7. Circle around 'X', triangle around 'Y' and square around 'Z'.
8. Curve as shown.
9. Four triangles inside one another.
10. Two Squares where shown.

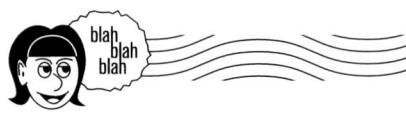 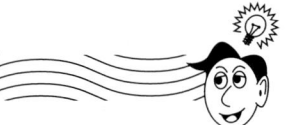

Exercise Two

Each pupil has a sheet of blank paper in front of him or her.

The teacher reads out each instruction twice.

Allow time between each instruction for the pupils to complete the required task(s).

It is useful if the pupils can not see one another's papers. However, it does not matter greatly as some instructions require different responses from different pupils.

Instructions:

1. Write your first name and the first and last letter of your middle name, at the bottom of the page, in the middle.

2. Circle the first letter of your middle name.

3. If you are wearing anything red, write the lower case letter 'r' under your name. Otherwise, write the capital letter 'T'.

4. Fold your page in half vertically. Reopen it and on the back of your page, rule two lines very close together on either side of the fold line.

5. Turn back to the front. In the right-hand half of the page, draw three circles arranged in the shape of a triangle, but not touching.

6. Using the numbers '2', '4' and '6', place one number in the centre of each circle.

7. Inside the circles, place a circle around the number six, a triangle around the number four and a square around the number two.

8. In the left half of the page, draw an angle which starts at the upper left-hand corner, comes down to touch the fold mark in the very centre of the page and continues to the bottom left-hand corner.

9. Within the angle and in the middle of the half page, draw four squares, one within the other. Then write the letter 'K' in the very centre square.

10. Outside the angle but within the left half page, draw two squares, one above and one below the point of the angle.

Exercise Two

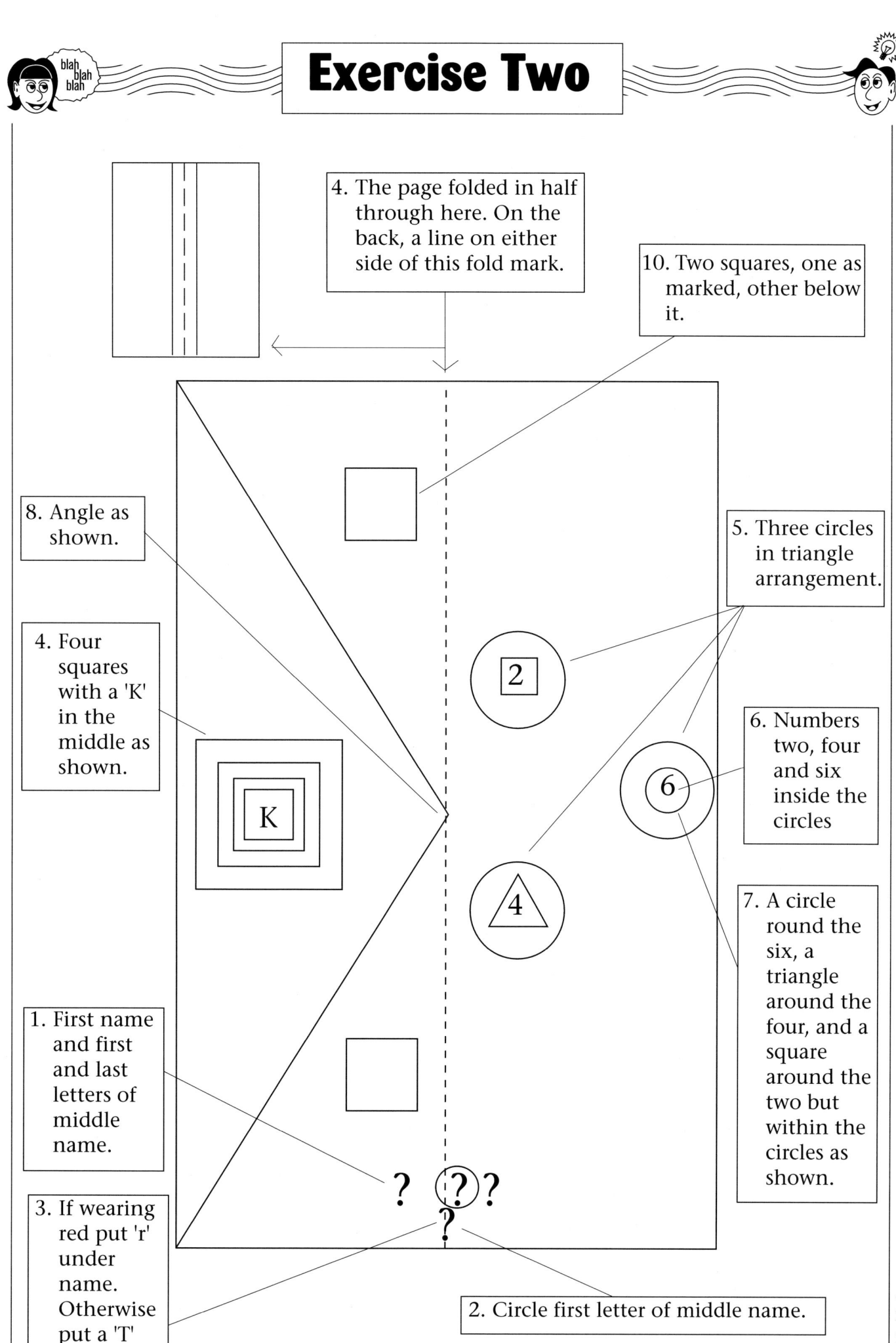

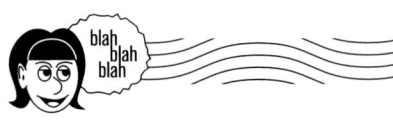

Exercise Three

Each pupil has a sheet of blank paper in front of him or her.

The teacher reads out each instruction twice.

Allow time between each instruction for the pupils to complete the required task(s).

It is useful if the pupils can not see one another's papers. However, it does not matter greatly as some instructions require different responses from different pupils.

Instruction:

1. Write the first letter of your first name and your whole last name at the top of the page, in the middle.

2. If you have black hair, draw a cross through the first letter of your last name. Otherwise, put a circle around it.

3. If you are wearing anything green, write the upper case letter 'G' below your name. Otherwise, write a lower case 'b'.

4. Fold your page in quarters, so each quarter is a rectangle of the same shape and there is a corner of the page in each quarter.

5. On the front of your sheet in the bottom left-hand corner, draw a circle.

6. Put a line of three dots down the middle of the circle and two dots across, forming a cross which shares the dot in the centre – a total of five dots.

7. Draw lines joining the four outer dots to form a diamond.

8. In the top right quarter, draw a set of three vertical lines intersected by a set of three horizontal lines. Write the number of squares formed below the drawing.

9. In the bottom right-hand corner, repeat the operation but with four lines each way instead of three. Write the number of squares formed above the drawing.

10. Finally, in the top left-hand quarter, draw the main compass lines. Label them using first letters only. Also label the points halfway between each, ensuring that you start with North pointing towards the top of the page.

Exercise Three

3. If wearing green, 'G' below name. Otherwise 'b'.

1. First letter of first name and whole last name.

2. If black hair, cross through first letter of last name. Otherwise circle it.

10. Compass points labelled as shown.

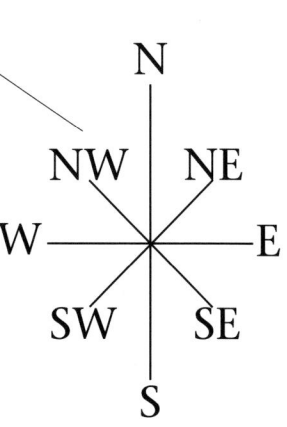

8. Three vertical lines crossed by three horizontal ones. Number of squares below.

4

5. Circle as shown.

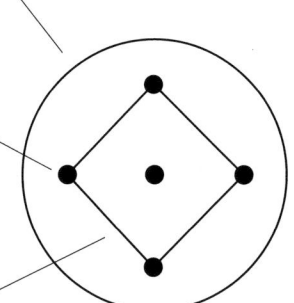

6. A line of 3 dots down and 2 across - total 5.

7. Lines drawn to form a diamond.

9

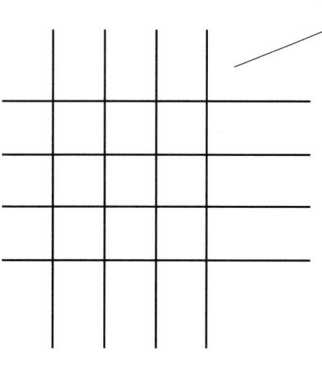

6. Four vertical lines crossed by four horizontal ones. Number of squares above.

4. Page folded into quarters as shown.

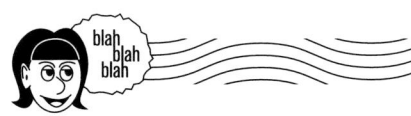
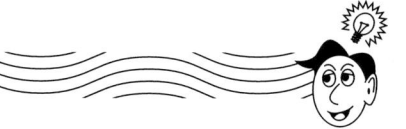

Exercise Four

Each pupil has a sheet of blank paper in front of him or her.

The teacher reads out each instruction twice.

Allow time between each instruction for the pupils to complete the required task(s).

It is useful if the pupils can not see one another's papers. However, it does not matter greatly as some instructions require different responses from different pupils.

Instructions:

1. Write the first letter of your first name, then every second letter of your middle name, at the top of the page, in the middle.

2. If you have red hair, draw a cross through the letter of your first name. Otherwise, draw a circle around it.

3. If you are wearing anything orange or red, write the letter 'Y' twice below your name. Otherwise write the letter 'N' three times before your name.

4. Fold your page in quarters horizontally so each quarter is a rectangle of the same shape, but so there are two corners of the page in two of the quarters and no corners in the middle quarters.

5. In the top quarter, draw three circles touching, arranged in the shape of a triangle.

6. Mark in the centre point of each circle with a heavy dot. Then connect the dots with straight lines to form a triangle.

7. In the third quarter from the top, draw a large square. Divide it into four smaller squares.

8. If your first name starts with the letter 'A', 'B', 'C', 'D', 'E', 'F', 'G', 'H' or 'I', draw a square in the second quarter from the top. If not, draw a circle.

9. In the bottom quarter, draw the shape which you did not draw from the previous instruction.

10. Link the circle and square with a line which travels around the three circles at the top of the page.

Exercise Four

3. 'YY' below name if wearing orange or red. Otherwise 'NNN' before the name.

2. If hair is red, draw a cross through first letter of first name. Otherwise, draw a circle around it.

1. First letter of first name then every second letter of middle name.

5. Three circles touching.

6. Centres marked and connected to form a triangle.

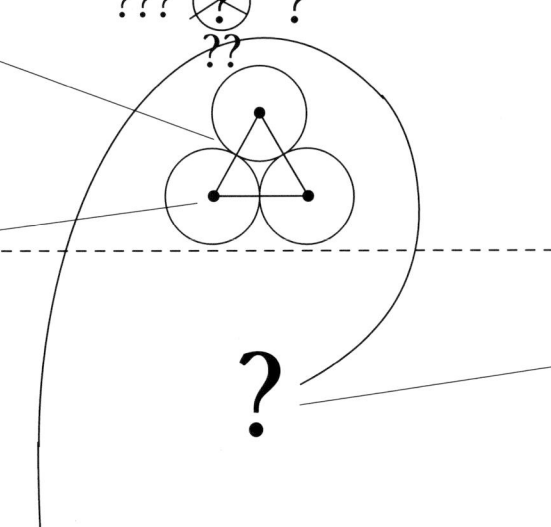

8. If first name starts with the letters 'A' to 'I', a square drawn here. Otherwise, a circle.

4. Folded in quarters as shown.

10. Shapes linked. Line goes around top circles as shown.

7. Large square divided into four smaller squares.

9. Either a circle or a square, whichever was not drawn in number 8.

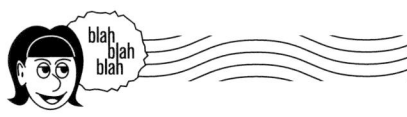 

Exercise Five

Each pupil has a sheet of blank paper in front of him or her.

The teacher reads out each instruction twice.

Allow time between each instruction for the pupils to complete the required task(s).

It is useful if the pupils can not see one another's papers. However, it does not matter greatly as some instructions require different responses from different pupils.

Instructions:

1. Write your first name, middle name and age backwards at the bottom of the page, on the right-hand side.

2. If you are wearing shoes, circle your middle name. If not, circle your first name.

3. If you are wearing anything yellow, pink or white, write the capital letter 'Y' twice at the top of the page, in the middle. If not, do the same thing with the capital letter 'N'.

4. Fold your page in quarters so each quarter is a rectangle of the same shape and there is a corner of the page in each quarter. Trace over the lines on the back of your sheet.

5. Turn to the front of your sheet and in the top right-hand quarter, draw a circle.

6. Put a smiley face on the circle, add some hair, a tiny stick figure body and two large ears sticking out the sides.

7. In the quarter diagonally opposite your smiling person, draw a large triangle which takes up most of the space.

8. If your last name starts with the letter 'J', 'K', 'L', 'M', 'N', 'O', 'P', or 'Q', draw a triangle in the top left-hand quarter. Otherwise, draw an oval.

9. If you are 10, 11 or 12 years old, write the numbers 1 to 10 backwards across the top of the bottom right quarter. Anyone else, write the numbers 1 to 10 forwards in the same space.

10. Rule a pair of diagonal lines through the entire page and write the letter 'C' at the point at which they intersect.

Exercise Five

3. If wearing yellow, pink or white, two 'Y's. Otherwise two 'N's.

4. Page folded into quarters as shown. Folds ruled over on back of page.

5. Circle

6. Smiley face, hair, small stick figure body and large ears.

8. If last name starts with the letters 'J' to 'Q', a triangle. Otherwise, an oval.

9. If aged 10 to 12, write 1 to 10 backwards. Other ages write 1 to 10 forwards.

10. Diagonals ruled in with the letter 'C' at the intersection.

2. If wearing shoes, circle second name. Otherwise, the first.

3. Large triangle.

1. First name, middle name and age written backwards.

Exercise Six

Each pupil has a sheet of blank paper in front of him or her.

The teacher reads out each instruction twice.

Allow time between each instruction for the pupils to complete the required task(s).

It is useful if the pupils can not see one another's papers. However, it does not matter greatly as some instructions require different responses from different pupils.

Instructions:

1. Write your first name and last name upside down at the top left of the page.

2. If you have brown hair, draw a cross through the last letter of your first name. If not, put a cross through the first letter of your last name.

3. If you are wearing a watch or earring, write a capital 'L' four times at the bottom of the page, in the middle. If you are not wearing either, do the same thing with a capital 'N'.

4. Fold your page in horizontal quarters so each rectangle is the same shape but so there are two rectangles with two corners and two with none. On the back of your sheet, trace over the lines you have created.

5. Turn back to the front of your sheet. In the bottom quarter of the sheet, draw three circles, not touching, arranged in a straight line.

6. Draw a line from the left of the page, going under the first circle, over the second circle, under the third and then across to the right side of the page.

7. Draw a mirror reflection of this drawing in the next quarter up, as if the mirror rested on the fold.

8. In the top quarter of the page, draw three squares and two circles, not touching, arranged in a straight horizontal line and with no square adjoining a square.

9. In the final quarter, draw two squares and three circles, not touching, arranged in a straight horizontal line and with no circle adjoining a circle.

10. Rule a zigzag line linking all the squares in the two upper quarters and another to link the circles.

Exercise Six

1. First and last name upside down.

2. For brown hair, cross through last letter of the first name. Others cross through first letter of last name.

8. Three squares and two circles as shown.

10. Zigzag lines as shown.

3. Two squares and three circles as shown.

4. Folded into quarters. Folds ruled over on back

7. Mirror reflection of lower quarter.

5. Three circles as shown.

6. Curved line as shown.

3. Wearing watch or earrings, draw four capital 'L's as shown. Otherwise, do the same with 'N's.

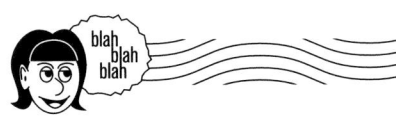

Exercise Seven

Each pupil has a sheet of blank paper in front of him or her.

The teacher reads out each instruction twice.

Allow time between each instruction for the pupils to complete the required task(s).

It is useful if the pupils can not see one another's papers. However, it does not matter greatly as some instructions require different responses from different pupils.

Instructions:

1. Write every second letter of your first name and last name, and your age at the bottom right of the page.

2. If you are not wearing shoes, circle your age and put a box around your name.

3. If you are not wearing a watch or earring, write the number '8' at both ends of your name. Otherwise, write '9'.

4. Fold your page in quarters so each quarter is a rectangle of the same shape and there is a corner of the page in each quarter. On the back of your sheet, rule two close parallel lines over each of the fold lines you made.

5. Turn to the front of your sheet and in the bottom right-hand quarter, draw three identical circles in a horizontal line which are not touching.

6. In between each of the three circles, draw a straight vertical line the length of the circles' diameter. Join these lines at the top and bottom to create a quadrilateral enclosing the centre circle.

7. In the centre circle draw three very small stars.

8. In the top right-hand quarter, draw a square intersected by a pair of diagonal lines. Below this square, write the number of triangles formed.

9. In the bottom left-hand corner, repeat the whole operation but with vertical and horizontal bisectors as well as diagonal lines.

10. Finally, in the top left-hand quarter, draw a large square and divide it into 16 smaller squares.

Exercise Seven

10. Square divided into sixteen smaller squares.

4. Fold sheet into quarters as marked. On back of sheet rule two close lines over each fold.

8. A square with diagonals. Number of triangles written below.

5. Three circles as shown.

6. Quadrilateral enclosing centre circle.

9. Square with diagonal, vertical and horizontal bisectors. Number of triangles written below.

7. Three stars in centre circle.

2. If not wearing shoes, circle age and box name.

3. If wearing a watch or earrings, write nine at the ends of name. Otherwise, write '8'.

1. Every second letter of your first and last name, then age.

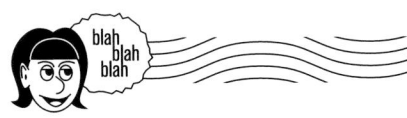

Exercise Eight

Each pupil has a sheet of blank paper in front of him or her.

The teacher reads out each instruction twice.

Allow time between each instruction for the pupils to complete the required task(s).

It is useful if the pupils can not see one another's papers. However, it does not matter greatly as some instructions require different responses from different pupils.

Instructions:

1. Write your first name in the top right-hand corner of the page and your last name in the bottom left-hand corner of the page.

2. If you are wearing any ties, clips or bands in your hair, draw a box around your last name.

3. If you are wearing shorts, write the letter 'S' in front of your last name. If you are wearing long pants, write the letter 'L', and if you are wearing something else, write the letter 'O'.

4. Fold your page in vertical quarters so each rectangle is the same shape but there are two corners of the page in two quarters and no corners in the other two quarters.

5. In the second quarter from the right, draw three circles in a vertical line.

6. Put a smiley face on the lower circle, an expressionless face on the middle circle and a frowning face on the upper circle.

7. Rule parallel lines approximately 5 mm apart from the top of the page, passing through the three circles to the bottom of the page. Draw a wavy line between the lines.

8. If your last name starts with a letter other than 'A', 'B', 'C', 'D', 'E', 'F', 'G', 'H' or 'I', draw a diamond in the second quarter from the left. If it does, draw a triangle.

9. In the very right quarter, draw the shape you did not draw from the previous instruction.

10. In the final quarter, draw three identical circles in a vertical line. Then, between the circles draw a straight horizontal line the length of the circles' diameter.

Exercise Eight

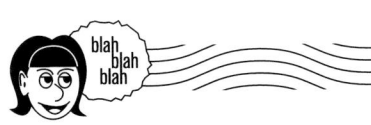

4. Folded into four vertically.

1. First name only at top right. Last name at bottom left.

5. Three circles arranged in a vertical line.

7. Parallel lines about 5 mm apart with wavy line in between.

6. Top circle frowning face, middle circle no expression, bottom circle smiling face.

10. Three circles in a vertical line. Horizontal lines to separate as shown.

9. The shape which was not drawn from instruction 8 – either triangle or diamond.

8. If last name starts with 'A' to 'I', a triangle in second quarter. Otherwise, draw a diamond.

3. If wearing shorts, 'S' in front of name. If wearing long pants, 'L', otherwise, 'O'.

2. If ties, clips or bands in hair, box around last name.

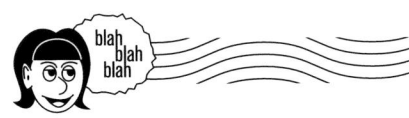

Exercise Nine

Each pupil has a sheet of blank paper in front of him or her.

The teacher reads out each instruction twice.

Allow time between each instruction for the pupils to complete the required task(s).

It is useful if the pupils can not see one another's papers. However, it does not matter greatly as some instructions require different responses from different pupils.

Instructions:

1. Write your first name in the bottom right-hand corner of the page and your last name in the top right-hand corner of the page.

2. If you are a boy, draw two lines under your last name. If you are a girl, draw three lines above your first name.

3. If you are wearing long pants, write 'L' at the end of your last name. If you are wearing shorts, write 'S' and if you are wearing something else, write 'O'.

4. Measure the length of your page. Now, fold it into horizontal thirds. On the back of your sheet, write the length of the paper and the width of each third.

5. Turn to the front of your sheet. In the middle third, draw a chain of five triangles which share a single straight line for a base and touch one another at the points.

6. Number the triangles in successive hundreds, starting at five hundred.

7. In the top third of the page, rule two diagonal lines, connecting the top corners to the points where the fold meets the edges of the paper.

8. In the lower third, draw a curved line which starts at the lower left-hand corner, comes up to touch the fold mark in the centre and then curves down to the bottom right-hand corner of the page.

9. Within the curve and in the middle of the third, draw four stick-figure people, one holding a bat, one a ball, one a stick and the last a flag.

10. Outside the curve but within the lower third, draw two more stick-figures, one on each side of the curve, both sitting watching the four.

Exercise Nine

7. Two diagonal lines crossing as shown.

1. First name at the bottom right and last name at top right.

3. If wearing long pants, write 'L' after last name. If wearing shorts, write 'S', and if wearing anything else, write 'O'

2. Boys put two lines under name. Girls see below.

6. Triangles numbered 500 to 900.

5. Five triangles with shared base.

4. Folded into thirds as shown. On the back, write the length of whole page and of each third

10. Two seated stick people where shown.

8. Curve as shown.

2. Girls put three lines above first name.

9. Four stick people with bat, ball, stick and flag under the curve.

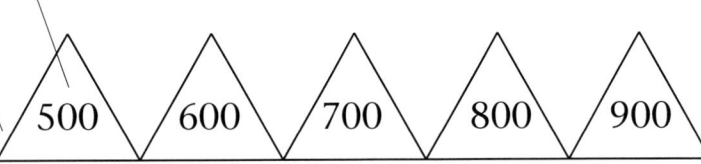

Listening Comprehension (Upper)

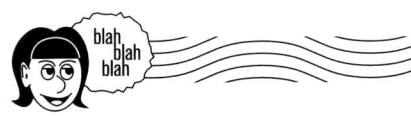

Exercise Ten

Each pupil has a sheet of blank paper in front of him or her.

The teacher reads out each instruction twice.

Allow time between each instruction for the pupils to complete the required task(s).

It is useful if the pupils can not see one another's papers. However, it does not matter greatly as some instructions require different responses from different pupils.

Instructions:

1. Write your first name in the top left-hand corner of the page, your last name in the top right-hand corner and your age in the bottom left-hand corner.

2. If you are a girl, draw two lines above your last name. If you are a boy, draw three lines beneath your last name.

3. If you are wearing a skirt, dress or culottes, write the letter 'D' over the top of your age. If you are wearing something else, write the letter 'E' beneath your age.

4. Measure the width of your page. Fold it into vertical thirds. Then, on the back of your sheet, write the width of your page and of each third.

5. Turn back to the front of your page and draw four horizontal wavy lines, close together, in the middle of the right-hand third.

6. Draw a butterfly above the wavy lines if you are a boy, and a fish below them if you are a girl.

7. Draw a beach ball in the space either directly above your butterfly or below your fish. Then, below all of these draw a watch.

8. In the centre third of the sheet, draw three triangles and two pentagons, arranged in a straight vertical line but not touching, and with no triangle next to another triangle.

9. In the left-hand third of the page, draw two triangles and three pentagons, arranged in a straight vertical line but not touching, and with no pentagon next to another pentagon.

10. Rule a zigzag line linking all of the triangles in the two thirds, and another to link all the pentagons.

Exercise Ten

1. First name here. Last name at top right. Age at bottom left.

4. Fold into vertical thirds as shown. On back of sheet, write width of page and of each third.

2. Girls: two lines over last name. Boys: three lines under.

6. Boys draw butterfly above wavy lines, girls draw fish below wavy lines.

8. Three triangles and two pentagons as shown in centre third.

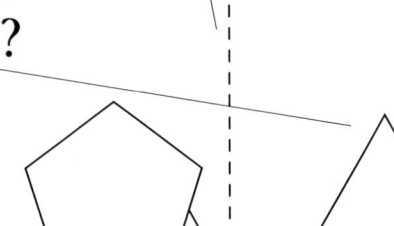

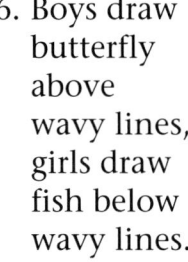

5. Four horizontal wavy lines.

9. Two triangles and three pentagons as shown in left third.

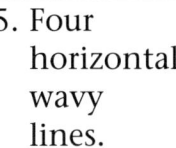

10. Zigzag links all triangles and all pentagons as shown.

7. Boys draw beach ball above butterfly. Girls draw one below fish. All draw a watch at the bottom of column.

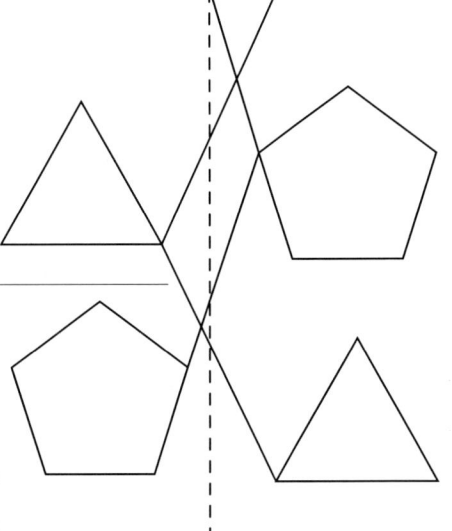

3. If wearing a skirt dress or culottes, 'D' over age. Otherwise, 'E' underneath age.

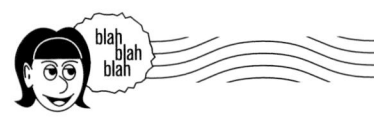

Exercise Eleven

Each pupil has a sheet of blank paper in front of him or her.

The teacher reads out each instruction twice.

Allow time between each instruction for the pupils to complete the required task(s).

It is useful if the pupils can not see one another's papers. However, it does not matter greatly as some instructions require different responses from different pupils.

Instructions:

1. Write your first name twice in the top left-hand corner of the page, your last name once in the top right-hand corner, and your age in the bottom left-hand corner.

2. Don't put a line under your last name on the right-hand side, or a circle around it. Don't put a cross through it either, but do all those to your first name once.

3. If your hair has any ties, bands or clips in it, write 'Yes' upside down under your last name. Otherwise, write 'No' the right way up above your last name.

4. Turn to the back of your page. Rule in the diagonals then fold your page along the lines. Put 'A' in the middle of two of the resulting triangles of the same shape, and 'B' in the other pair.

5. Turn back to the front of your page. At the top of the top triangle, draw four horizontal wavy lines, close together. Below the wavy lines, draw a circle with a triangle inside it and the letter 't' inside the triangle.

6. Below the circle but still in the top triangle, draw a small group of three stick-figure people standing on the roof of a house.

7. In the centre of the right-hand triangle, draw a small star, surrounded by five small circles and four small squares.

8. Draw a line connecting the star to your age and another connecting the triangle to your last name.

9. In the left-hand triangle, draw a stick-figure person with a rope leading to the hand of one of the stick-figure people on the roof.

10. Write your birthday month in the bottom triangle and draw a line joining it to your first name.

Exercise Eleven

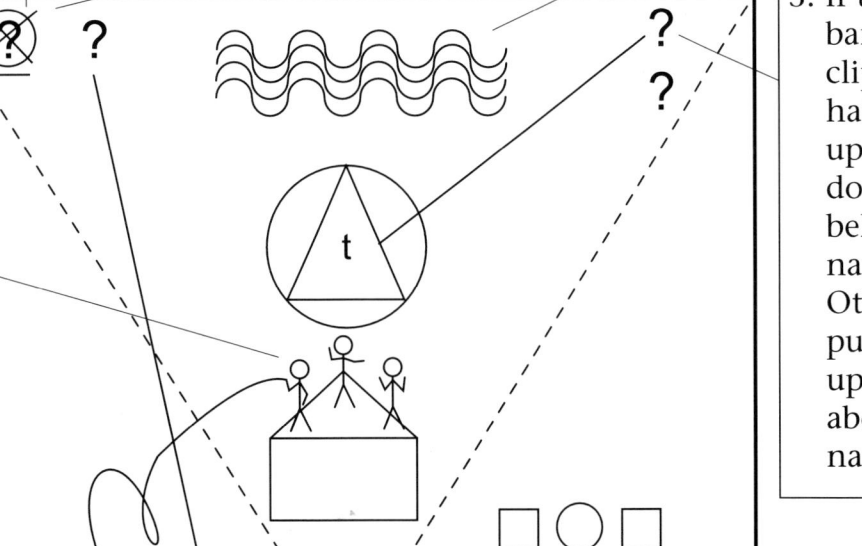

1. First name twice top left. Last name once top right. Age bottom left.

2. Line under, cross through and circle around first name.

3. If ties, bands or clips in hair, 'Yes' upside down below last name. Otherwise, put 'No' upright above last name.

4. Diagonals ruled on back and folded. Letters on back as shown.

5. Wavy lines as shown. Circle below with triangle inside and 't' inside that.

6. Three stick-figure people standing on a house.

7. Star in centre. Five circles and four squares around it

8. Lines from star to age and from triangle to last name.

9. Stick-figure with rope to one of the figures on the house.

10. Birthday month bottom triangle. Joined by line to first name.

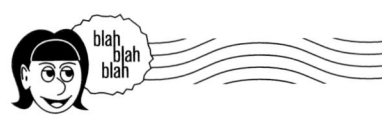

Exercise Twelve

Each pupil has a sheet of blank paper in front of him or her.

The teacher reads out each instruction twice.

Allow time between each instruction for the pupils to complete the required task(s).

It is useful if the pupils can not see one another's papers. However, it does not matter greatly as some instructions require different responses from different pupils.

Instructions:

1. Write your first name twice, once in each top corner of the page. Then write your last name in the bottom left-hand corner and your age in the bottom right-hand corner.

2. Put a line under your last name, a circle round your first name on the right and a cross through your first name on the left.

3. If your hair has no ties, bands or clips in it, write 'no' under your first name on the right. Otherwise, write 'yes' in the same place.

4. Turn your page over, rule in the diagonals and then fold along those lines. Label the four triangles formed 'W', 'X', 'Y', 'Z' so that 'W' and 'X' are the same shape, as are 'Y' and 'Z'.

5. Turn to the front. To the left of the right-hand side triangle, draw four horizontal wavy lines close together. To the right of the wavy lines, draw a circle around a triangle with the letter 'Z' inside it.

6. Above the circle but still within the quarter, draw a second circle and triangle just like the first one, but with the first letter of your last name inside the triangle.

7. To the right of this last circle, draw a small star and to the left of it, a small moon. Then draw a line running above the circle which connects the star to the moon.

8. Draw four horizontal wavy lines close together in the middle of the left-hand quarter.

9. If you are a girl, draw a butterfly above the wavy lines, and if you are a boy, draw a fish below them.

10. Draw a beach ball in the space directly to the right of the wavy lines and a watch in the space to the left.

Exercise Twelve

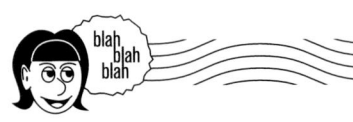

1. First name in each top corner. Last name at bottom left. Age at bottom right corner.

2. Line under last name (bottom left). Circle around first name on right. Cross through first name on left.

3. If wearing ties, clips or bands in hair, write 'Yes' under name here. Otherwise, 'No'.

9. Girls: butterfly above wavy lines. Boys: fish below wavy lines.

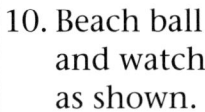

8. Four wavy lines as shown.

10. Beach ball and watch as shown.

4. Diagonals ruled on back then folded. Four triangles formed, labelled as shown.

6. Second circle with triangle and first letter of last name inside.

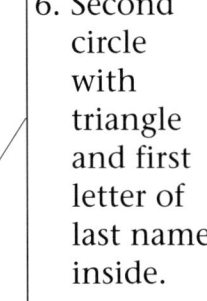

7. Star and moon as shown with line to connect.

5. Wavy lines as shown. Circle to right of wavy lines with triangle and 'Z' inside.

Listening Comprehension (Upper)

My Listening Success Graph

Name. . . . .

Score

Exercise

My Listening Success Graph

Name. . . . .

Score

Exercise